FINDING THE
LIGHT

The Magical Story of the
First Chanukah in America
& much more

Arthur Piccolo

Dear Heidi,

with my
Best wishes!

Arthur
9/2021

TABLE OF CONTENTS

DEDICATION

John E. Herzog

He stands alone in his own way

here at Bowling Green

he now is gone to other shores

he is still here always will

his presence felt all the time

especially by me !

he stands for something far more

than his successes it is what he

did and does stands for so much more

others know as well as I

there is no mystery it is widely known

may others learn what John

long has known

history and community

makes us far better all of us

our Spirits will live on

long after we are gone

SPECIAL ACKNOWLEDGEMENTS

Below are a special group of individuals beyond the dedication of this book to John Herzog and who are among an even larger group who I am grateful for the contributions they have made to Bowling Green that are reflected one way or another in some cases many ways in this new book.

Philip Altheim. I first met Philip in the mid-1990s when I was in desperate need of more assistance to fund the expensive annual then very large Christmas Tree at Bowling Green. Philip was at the time President of a large electrical company Forest Electric. Philip's generosity became almost endless in support of this project as long as he was President of the Company and he did more than anyone to keep that project alive for years. There is more the Menorah he funded named now in his honor The Philip Altheim Menorah you will read about in the pages of this book.

Rabbi Joseph Potasnik. Rabbi Potasnik's strong support for celebrating Chanukah at Bowling Green since we began to do so in 1997 and his enthusiasm for early Jewish American history here has been instrumental. It is why along with his many other accomplishments and titles as New York's Rabbi, Joseph Potasnik is also the 'official' Rabbi of Bowling Green.

Rabbi Nissi Eber. Decades younger than Rabbi Potasnik and more recent to Bowling Green, Rabbi Eber lives near Bowling Green and his interest in Chanukah at Bowling Green has also been inspirational. Most of all Rabbi Eber and his group The Jewish Learning Experience funded the Circle of Light in December 2020 which is now the permanent tribute to the First Jews to arrive in North America that finally exists to honor them.

Mendy Braun & Yehuda Feder. Mendy and Yehuda manage 11 Broadway among other properties. This is the building where Bowling Green Association has resided for the last 6 years and where I have written this and other books. They have maintained and installed the Bowling Green Menorah year after year among their other support.

Scott Rechler. Scott is one of the most important business leaders in New York City and founder & CEO of a major real estate company RXR. Scott's support for both the Chanukah and Christmas projects in recent years has been generous. Others should show as much community spirit as Scott does.

Koeppel Family. Alfred, Caleb, and David Koeppel who owned 26 Broadway for many years played a pivotal role in the creation of the Bowling Green Association in 1987 and provided office space for many years as well for as long as they owned 26 Broadway. None of these projects included those portrayed in this book without having their early frequent support.

Arturo DiModica. Arturo who passed away early in 2021 most famously is responsible for his 3 ½ ton bronze "Charging Bull" which forevermore will define Bowling Green and has since December 1989, the greatest gift of art ever given to New York City as a result of Arturo's generosity. In the context of this book Arturo created the first Menorah ever displayed in Bowling Green, back in 1997. A magnificent 14 ft. tall work of impressive sculpture.

Tom Cummins & Andy Carson. The two Forest Electric electricians who worked for Philip Altheim and in one very remarkable Chanukah story these two Irish Americans in just one week just in time for Chanukah designed and created the current Bowling Green Menorah in 2005 from off the shelf electrical components. This story and their Menorah are 'legendary.'

Kamil Kubik. The now deceased impressionist painter best known for his New York City landscape paintings who back in 1997 painted an oil "First Night of Chanukah" that has permanently memorialized in a spectacular way the first time Chanukah was ever formally celebrated at Bowling Green and the lighting of Arturo DiModica's sculptural bronze Menorah that night.

Ibrahim Kurtulus. Ibrahim is the long time vice chairman of the Bowling Green Association and deeply involved here in Lower Manhattan. Specific to this book and Chanukah at Bowling Green, Ibrahim introduced me to Rabbi Joseph Potasnik many years ago to my continuing appreciation.

The Unnamed. There are many others over almost 40 years who have come and gone in the context of Bowling Green generally and the Chanukah project specifically who are not named here by me but who also deserve my thanks.

INTRODUCTION

For much of my life I had no idea who they were nor when or why the First Jews arrived in North America. Most Americans including many American Jews still do not know. Why do I care ? Why should you care ?

I became aware back in 1997 in my investigations of the history of Lower Manhattan generally and Bowling Green specifically as founder of the Bowling Green Association. Once I did I discovered a fascinating and important story about early American history. It has culminated in this new book by me almost 25 years later.

A total of 24 Jewish men, women and children arrived here then tiny New Amsterdam in late summer 1654. 23 of them came here fleeing persecution in South America. One was sent here by successful Jews in Amsterdam to determine if New Amsterdam would be a good place for Jews to settle.

Theirs is both a quintessential American story and just as much as a Jewish story. Combined their story reaches mythic proportions and a story for the ages everyone should know and savor for its richness and importance.

In Part One I transform their adventure into a magical story about the First Chanukah in America. I call it a children's story but as with all memorable children's stories they appeal to adults as much as children.

Part Two is a more detailed history of both Lower Manhattan and Bowling Green and more details about the First Jews to arrive here in 1654. And how we have celebrated Chanukah here beginning December 1997 and ever since.

Part Three is an image portfolio with commentary about all this.

I hope you will join me in these pages in a journey of discovery, and why it is America's Chanukah story reminiscent of the original Chanukah long ago.

PART ONE

FINDING

THE

LIGHT

America's First

Chanukah Story

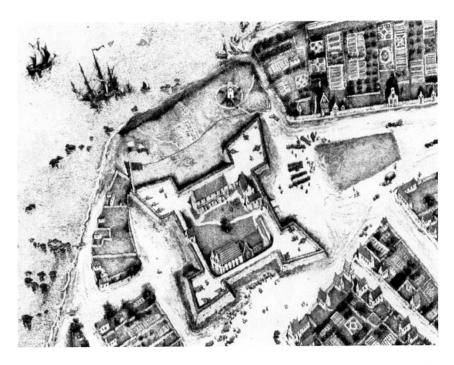

The First Jews to come to North America arrived on a ship as shown

here in the upper left corner of this illustration of the center of

New Amsterdam at the time of their arrival in 1654.

Fort Amsterdam in the center was where they went to get

permission from Director General Peter Stuyvesant to stay.

Right in front of the fort was the "town square" of

New Amsterdam where everyone met and traded goods.

PETER STUYVESANT

FINDING THE LIGHT

Chapter 1

Jacob Barsimson did not know where he was. But he knew he had been here before. Something was familiar.

When he heard the signing coming from the Darkness then Jacob began to remember. But who were all these people dressed in strange clothes surrounding him. Why didn't they seem to see him. As the sky darkened and the voices grew louder the others coming out of the Darkness. Now he could see them. At least they were dressed like him. How many of them were there. It seemed like a lot. Men, women, children.

They were like a great swaying mass of people. Moving in rhythm to the Jewish song they were singing. Barsimson also noticed the fence surrounding him as these Jews YES Jews men, women and children walked through the gate and began spreading out as they entered. They all looked as confused as he was. Where were they ? Who were they ?

They walked around even through all those people in other strange clothes surrounding him. Jacob realized what he had just said. They walked "through" those people surrounding him. Something what surely wrong. How could that be.

Who are they. Who am I ? Am I one of them. This crowd doesn't see them either. Jacob turned round the whole scene became even stranger. He saw shining buildings all around him. Radiating light from their windows high into the sky.

At that point these other Jews if that is what they were because Jacob was not sure of anything at this point they all joined Jacob high above the others these strangers surrounding them in the middle of this Circle this stage. And now he could count them. There were 23 men, women, and children and one of them seemed to be their leader. A tall thin man with a beard, some gray in his hair, wearing a long black coat, a white shirt buttoned to his neck, and most noticeable of all a black hat that framed his face wonderfully and somehow seemed to glow.

Then he approached Jacob. " Good to see you again my brother." "Whaaaat do I know you." The other man said, "Of course you do Jacob let's see how many years is it now since 1654 ...." Once again Jacob said " whaaaaat."

" Jacob it must be old age your mind is slipping. You know who I am Asser ..... Asser Levy ... we first met right here on this very spot back on September 7, 1654, and years later we all made a solemn vow to return here every year at Chanukah forever more as Spirits to remember always remember who we are and what we accomplished ..... together."

Then Jacob leapt with joy "YES YES YES .. how could I ever forget .. my dear dear friend Asser and all of you ... we are together again."

Together they were. As they had gathered here every December for the eight nights of Chanukah for a very long time now.

Just as they had vowed to do in life when back in 1654 and the years that followed Asser Levy, Jacob Barsimson and the others were the first Jews here in North America when this place was called New Amsterdam. Now the fun was about to begin. There was a reason a huge crowd stood filling this place this circle surrounded by an iron fence and so excited to see these 24 Jews in their midst.

It was the legend of Chanukah at Bowling Green. On this First Night of Chanukah early in the 21st century. Hundreds of years after Jacob, Asser and the other 22 had completed their Earthly journeys to go over to the Other Side they have continued to return.

Their Spirits have been returning here every December since 1776. More about that later. What you need to know right now is that since then each December at Chanukah all 24 come to life become visible to those alive right now. These 24 Jews have come backs to lead the most wonderful Chanukah celebration anywhere.

A simple elegant large golden Menorah appears exactly in the center of what is a fountain in warm weather in the middle of this park, each December for Chanukah. That is why there are so many people here tonight. It is the First Night of Chanukah. The legend of the First Jews draws

Jews and non-Jews from all over each year to witness this Miracle for 8 consecutive nights.

It was fully dark now. The sun had set completely on its journey westward taking all its light with it. And then it happened. As it has the Eight Nights of Chanukah for more than 200 years. An unearthly glow beautiful mesmerizing beyond what words can describe radiates out of the Darkness where the Spirits of Asser, Jacob and the others stand above this crowd surrounding them on every side wildly excited for what they were witnessing.

In an instant they are here again their bodies just as they were back in 1654 are returned to them. Nobody fully understands how. Not them. Not the crowd. Not the scientists and sages who have studied what the grown up world called an unexplained phenomenon. The crowd stands there in hushed silence. The 24 Jews up there above them all look surprised and delighted they do every Chanukah.

It takes a few moments for them to orient themselves. To remember what it was like to be here back in the 1600s. Then they look at each other knowingly in the joy that binds them together as Jews for all time. They smile at each other. They hug. Then it begins. What many call the "ritual" everyone else has come to see. Better to witness and never forget this magical moment.

Music glorious music fills the air radiates throughout the crowd. And these 24 Spirits made real to the crowd tonight begin a joyous dance all the women, the children, the men in a large circle dancing and singing with a power and majesty that no mere mortals ever could. All around the great glowing Menorah in the center. They dance and sing until all the thousands and thousands more who have filled this plaza are dancing and singing along with them.

When the music ends the 23 who had been carrying lanterns in the Darkness place them symmetrically at the edge of this circular stage above the crowd. Jacob who does not have a lantern carries an ornately carved rod taller than him.

Finally as those who are in the crowd who return here year after year know and as the others know because all that happens here each Chanukah is so famous there is almost no one in the world who does not know the story of what happens each year at Chanukah at Bowling Green.

Chapter 2

Now it's time to hear the story that never grows old from the lips of those who were here how the First Jews came here. The beginning of the Jewish presence in America. Jacob and Asser tell the very same story every year but each year it sounds new again even more that Jacob and Asser tell it as though it was happening right now. You could say it is.

Because what happens next is that Jacob waves his rod call it a magic wand if you like. He circles the stage and waves it over the crowd. Some who have seen it say they are reminded of Moses parting the waters with his staff. Anyway as Jacob waves his rod above the crowd sparks of light spread throughout what is now a park. Everyone there enters a trance which takes them all back to 1654. August 22, 1654, the day Jacob Barsimson first set foot here in America .

Now everyone was back in 1654 in Nieuw Amsterdam or at least thought they were in this trance Jacob had created for them. And Jacob and Asser were about to tell them a story much like the original story of Chanukah more than 2000 years ago. This story America's Chanukah story another to likewise live throughout history about Light and a victory over oppression and discord.

Jacob spoke first as his eyes moved throughout the crowd and saw theirs twinkling like a million stars wanting to learn the Truth.

Then he began to speak with his baritone voice, "I was here first. I came here to New Amsterdam sent to survey this new city which was spoken of back in Amsterdam the large city in Europe this new city was named for. I was sent by Jewish leaders there successful businessmen eager for a place in this new land of America where Jews could settle and prosper."

" And so after a long ocean journey on a ship named the Pear Tree which I shared with goats and cows and other animals bound for this new world and lots of non-Jews coming to America to find a better life."

" I remember the day clearly it could have been yesterday our ship sailed into this enormous harbor, lush vegetation, trees and grasslands filling the shore. The water below us was crystal clear and schools of fish passed by the ship again and again. I even saw a pair of dolphin leap high in the sky."

" Most of all in the distance on this bright hot summer day as I stood at the very tip of the ship I could see small buildings and one larger, and it looked like people walking about although at first they were so small I was not sure. And in this vast body of water closer to the ship there were canoes some with one, others with a few strangely dressed men their faces painted. I had heard about them. Back in Europe they were called Indians."

Jacob continued his voice filed with excitement. Everyone listening all of them in a trance felt like they were there with him in August 1654 on the ship coming toward the small city New Amsterdam a bustling new trading colony with a growing reputation.

" Then finally our ship ever so slowly the sails lowered by the crew we came close to shore at the tip of what seemed like it was an island and the anchor was lowered. After some instructions from the captain to his crew about behaving themselves and that they had many more ports to visit back in Europe, those of us leaving were lowered into a small boat and rowed to shore. After us same the goats and the cows not easy to do."

" At the water's edge I stepped into a few inches of water and made my way past a small windmill which reminded me of home and toward a small group of curious men and women there to greet the arrival of our ship. I knew no one there. By their dress it was clear to me none of them were Jews."

" As I looked about in wonderment finally seeing New Amsterdam after hearing so much about it. It wasn't a moment later that a man carrying a musket and wearing what looked like a uniform came up to me and said ," I see you got off that ship the Pear Tree. All visitors must present themselves to our Director General Peter Stuyvesant. Follow me into the fort right here and right now."

" I was certainly not going to resist him and I knew the procedure. I was prepared. I carried with me a letter of introduction officially signed by important people back in Amsterdam. And stating that I was here for a period of time to report back on the conditions here whether or not Jewish settlers should come to New Amsterdam and make it their new home in this New World."

At that moment remembering himself and where he really was now hundreds of years later Jacob asked the crowd to turn around and look at the stately marble building to their south only yards beyond the park where they all stood.

" There RIGHT THERE that is exactly where the fort stood it was called Fort Amsterdam not anywhere as impressive as this building now the Alexander Hamilton U.S. Custom House as you see a very impressive U.S. government building."

" It was the symbol of authority in New Amsterdam also to protect this city more like a small village if someone tried to make trouble possibly the British who had other colonies not far away. So the big doors to the fort right there where the stairs are now the doors were opened on command of the soldier accompanying me."

" Inside it was quite large a group of wooden houses and some other wooden buildings. I was directed toward the largest and best looking building and told to wait outside. As I did with my large bag with all my possessions and my precious letter of introduction clutched in my hand as if it was a piece of gold. "

" I waited and waited in the hot sun as it rose higher and higher in the sky. It seemed like I was there for hours. Someone was nice enough to give me a cup of water as I began to feel weak from my weeks of travel. Finally the unfriendly soldier emerged from inside and walked up to me.

" Leave your bag here. His Excellency will see you now."

" Once inside I saw an enormous man seated behind a huge desk and a very large dog beside him. Without looking up he said, " So you are Barsimson, Jacob Barsimson I knew you were coming I received word some weeks ago. I have a letter from the director of my company back in Amsterdam. Give me your papers I was told you would have an official letter of introduction asking me to allow you to stay here for a brief time. Do you have such a letter Mr. Barsimson ? "

" Yes your Excellency it is right here. Finally Peter Stuyvesant looked up and I saw his face and those eyes for the first time. It was not a friendly look. It was obvious he was not happy to see me. It was very very clear to me. "

" Barsimson this looks official enough. But I can tell you you are wasting your time. You made a very long journey for nothing. I am sure after a short time here you will report back to your Jewish masters he said in a scowling sort of way that New Amsterdam is not a good place for Jews to settle."

" All my people are God fearing Christians and they don't like outsiders among them. Whether they are the British who are not true Christians, nor those who worship the Catholic Pope in Rome, or Jews who are non-believers."

" Jews will do better continuing to settle in Brazil and other places. Better even stay in Europe where they belong. That will be all Barsimson. Here take your letter. Behave yourself while you are here. My men will be watching. And remember here in New Amsterdam we observe the Sabbath on Sunday. Saturdays are normal working days here. Act accordingly."

Jacob could not have been more relieved to be done with this angry man. He had hoped to see his peg leg the one everyone talked about but he never rose from his seat.

Back outside the fort in front of it where lots of people were going about their business Jacob began to feel much better. As he stood there he realized that right in front of the fort was the bustling trading center of this town with the shoreline only a short distance away. There was so much activity on this flat sandy plain with the fort looming over it. Jacob felt much more at home there.

It was exactly where Jacob stood now in the middle of this large crowd now hundreds of years later. But with everyone entranced by his words they all believed they were back there with him in New Amsterdam on the afternoon of August 22, 1654. Jacob saw it and they could see in their minds what Jacob saw way back then.

There were a few Dutch soldiers practicing their marching back and forth, back and forth. There were women selling fresh vegetables, others selling fish from the harbor, and one man beaver skins. There were children running around having a grand time, small groups of men talking business it seems. It was quite a scene even joyous in a simple way and so much different than the stifling atmosphere inside the fort with Peter Stuyvesant.

All of a sudden there was a voice behind him "Welcome stranger I see you arrived on the Pear Tree today and it looks like you have just come from seeing Old Stuyvesant. I bet he scared you didn't he." Jacob turned round himself to greet this stranger.

" Good day my name is Jacob Barsimson and I've come from Amsterdam. And yes Stuyvesant is a rather frightening individual. And who are you sir. My name is Adriaen van der Donck and I am a member of the Council the Common Council of New Amsterdam, and it's a pleasure to meet you. I only recently returned myself from Europe and Amsterdam."

Jacob replied. " Nice to meet you sir but what is this Council. I had heard nothing about a Common Council."

" That's not surprising. May I call you Jacob ? Jacob our Peter Stuyvesant is doing all he can to keep it quiet. But it is different here now then it was before February 2nd of last year. We've got our charter now to govern ourselves. We don't all work for Old Peg Leg and his masters the Dutch West India Company anymore."

"Yes Stuyvesant still has the fort and the soldiers. We still must call him Director General. He has more power than anyone else but it is different now much different. We have our rights. More about that later. Right now you need a place to say while you're here."

With that Jacob picked up his heavy bag and his new friend who impressed Jacob so much more than Stuyvesant introduced him to a local inn keeper right there on what was called Broad Way and Jacob found a place to stay.

Chapter 3

Jacob found himself a cozy little room on their second floor of one of the few inns in New Amsterdam that catered to travelers. He had a good view of the fort and the inviting space in front of it where he first set foot here that was always abuzz with activity.

The inn was right on the Broad Way the unpaved central road that led from the fort north past the town into the unknown where for some danger lurked. For others the land beyond the town was a wonderland of exotic animals, wild trees, freshwater brooks, all kinds of fruits growing wild, fragrant flowers, beautiful meadows and the sky filled with birds of every color singing enchanting songs. Jacob was happy enough hearing about that wonderland from others. He stayed inside the small town.

He confined himself to the town south of the stockade wood wall that stretched from one river to the other and marked the northern boundary of New Amsterdam. For the next two weeks Jacob Barsimson spent his days with his Bible, notebook and pen in hand walking these unfamiliar streets, speaking with everyone, and jotting down note after note. His impressions of New Amsterdam and its people. Jacob would be making a favorable report.

After all that is why he was sent here by Jewish leaders in Amsterdam to find out if New Amster-dam would be a good place for Jews to settle in this New World. Would they be welcome. Are there opportunities here for Jews to worship and to prosper as Jews and as merchants and trades people. Just as more and more Jews were doing freely back in Amsterdam if no where else in Europe.

One place Jacob Barsimson stayed away from was the inside of the fort and the one person he avoided at all costs was the Director General Peter Stuyvesant. Jacob already knew part of his report would say that Stuyvesant was one reason for Jews to stay away. At the same time Jacob was a wise Jew who had faced others like Stuyvesant all his life. Neither he or those who sent him here were going to allow a few bad apples to be enough to stop Jews from coming here if there were other reasons why Jews might flourish in New Amsterdam. Not when Jews had almost 3000 years of history even beginning before Moses of facing oppressors and overcoming them. The only good thing Jacob Barsimson could say about Peter Stuyvesant is that Jews had dealt with a lot worse in other places in other times and right now. They could survive Peter Stuyvesant.

So it was that Jacob spent his days going here and there. While many different languages were spoken in New Amsterdam which had begun attracting people from all over the globe as its reputation grew as a good place to do business in the New World. Dutch was the dominant language since this was a Dutch colony. Everyone learned enough Dutch in addition to using their hands, eyes and movements to communicate well enough with everyone else.

So while Jacob heard French, German, Polish, English, Swedish, African and American Indian languages spoken in New Amsterdam he could talk with everyone more or less. Jacob spoke Dutch. He was from the Netherlands Dutch being his language made it that much easier for him to fully appreciate New Amsterdam.

Having arrived on August 22, 1654, Barsimson was here as the days began to grow shorter and cool sea breezes began to make the hot summer days more pleasant and the colonists began to speak of Fall only weeks away. Jacob began to think of the High Holy Days. That for the first time in his life he would be alone without any other Jews anywhere in this new land. Not in New Amsterdam but not in any of the other colonies springing up all over this New World. And while nobody else seemed to care Jacob knew he was the first Observant Jew ever to come to America. North America anyway there were some thriving and some troubled Jewish colonies already in South America.

" So how are you today Mr. Gehring how are your crops coming along." " Good to see you again Sarah how are the children." " Pierre the bread you bake is the best in the world." So it was as September began Jacob Barsimson came to know almost everyone in town. Not everyone. Stuyvesant was not the only person in New Amsterdam who was not excited to see a Jew. Luckily those like Stuyvesant were few and Jacob learned who to avoid so as not to ruin his day or his purpose being here.

On Saturdays he would spend most of the day alone in his room and sitting by the shore among the leafy trees towering over him by the river saying prayers, singing hymns, reading from his Bible. Jacob made believe he was back in Amsterdam sitting in the central Synagogue seated among hundreds of other Jews who were at home back in Amsterdam where they could live openly as Jews.

By now Jacob Barsimson had a secret which he wanted to share with his Congregation back home. He could see himself invited to the podium by Rabbi Katz at the end of the Service to announce he had just returned from New Amsterdam. That while it was not a perfect place for Jews and that there would be some challenges. Still it was a land filled with opportunities. With the blessing of Jewish leaders he was going to lead a group of Jewish settlers back to New Amsterdam. With them make his new home there. Build America's first Synagogue. Yes he was dreaming again.

Then as thought he had been in a trance his mind brought him back to where he really was as he heard a booming voice "Jacob how are you." It was Adriaen van der Donck who he met his first day in New Amsterdam who helped

Jacob find a place to stay. " Good to see you my friend always good to see you."

Jacob had learned much more about Adriaen in the few weeks he had been in New Amsterdam even though Adriaen himself had left the enclosed village to return to his home up north on the other side of the wall. Adriaen van der Donck was considered the hero of New Amsterdam by everyone. He was the leader they needed.

Adriaen had led what might be called a revolt a few years earlier. He headed the group that wanted New Amsterdam free of the tyrannical rule of Stuyvesant and the company that owned the town the Dutch West India Company.

Adriaen van der Donck and the others wanted a free independent city where those living there made the rules not some unsympathetic master sitting high and mighty in the fort. It was quite a struggle it went on and on. They did not give up.

Finally Adriaen van der Donck set sail back to Europe and old Amsterdam with a petition signed by most of the colony imploring those in charge back home to give them their freedom. With all his strength and tireless efforts the Burgomasters in Amsterdam said yes. We will provide you a charter much like our own. And so New Amsterdam became mostly free of the Dutch West India Company on February 2, 1653. The first self-governing place in all of America. With a Council, and elections and their own judges.

Chapter 4

They were almost free that is. Peter Stuyvesant the Director General still had much of his power because he controlled the fort, much of the land, and the services the town needed to protect itself. He still controlled those who came and went. As Jacob Barsimson knew only too well from his own experience.

" Adriaen I am glad to see you again. I have some news. I will be leaving. Returning to Amsterdam as soon as another ship arrives headed back to Europe."

" No Jacob stay with us make a home for yourself. This land is wondrous bountiful. There is so much more here than in Europe. America is where the future lies and I am sure New Amsterdam will grow to become one of the great cities in America. And don't worry about Peter Stuyvesant he will be gone soon, and we won't stand for any more like him ever again."

"That's very kind of you Adriaen but my job was to come then report back to the Jewish leaders in Amsterdam. Besides it is lonely for me here. Almost everyone is friendly but it's not the same without other Jews, without Sabbath services, and now with the High Holy Days approaching. But I do have some good news. I am going to report that New Amsterdam would make a good place for Jews to settle in America. I hope to lead a group back and stay ."

Then they spoke for hours and hours by the shore. A gentle sun overhead punctuated by passing puffy clouds. A sea breeze cooling them. Birds overhead. Fish leaping out of the harbor before them. They were in Paradise. Jacob learned much about the history of this place he did not know from Adriaen van der Donck. All the way back to Captain Adriaen Block who was the first European ever to set foot on this island of Manna-hata the Indian name for their island. Block arrived back in November 1613 before anyone else.

Jacob learned from Adriaen while Block and his men were exploring this exotic unchartered island their ship burned along with all their possessions and provisions. They were left stranded without anyone to rescue them. They should have all died on this island that winter. Instead the local Natives helped them build huts for themselves not far from where Jacob and Adriaen were sitting and talking. Block and his men built those huts right on what would be Broad Way and only yards north of where the fort would stand. None of which Block could have imagined seeing back in 1613.

The Indians gave Block and his men clothes for the cold winter and fruits, nuts and vegetables, and Block's men hunted deer and bear and other animals so plentiful on the island. After the long winter Block's men and Indians helping them they built Block a new ship. Block and his crew sailed on to explore other places before returning home. Block named a small island for himself Block Island. That was 41 years ago but the story still inspired everyone.

With that story Adriaen van der Donck and Jacob Barsimson parted ways. Bidding each other farewell for now. Jacob watched as Adriaen got in his canoe to paddle up the North River to his home far outside of the town. Jacob would not learn until later this was the last time he would ever see Adriaen as the rays of the late afternoon sun made a golden pathway on the river's surface. As van der Donck passed through it he glowed like a god from another world. Sadly soon after he would be killed in an altercation with some Native Indians. But he would not be forgotten.

As August turned into September Jacob scanned the grand harbor waiting ever more eagerly for the next billowing white sails he would see coming out of the distance. The ship that he would board to begin his long ocean journey back to Amsterdam and the Jewish community that had sent him on this journey of Discovery.

Not that Jacob Barsimson was bored. Not in the least.

While he wandered around the town river to river and as far north as the Wall, stopping in shops, savoring the smell of freshly baked bread. Listening to the chatter coming from the town's many taverns, but never entering them, the place where Jacob always gravitated and spent so much of his time was the place everyone called The Plaine, the area right in front of the fort, what we would call the town square. It bordered the shoreline. You could taste the harbor breeze. Watch the fishermen come and go and children splashing at the water's edge as their mothers kept a watchful eye.

It was a place of never ending activity, where the settlers and the Native Indians mingled, and sometimes fought, where all sorts of deals were made, produce, and fish, furs, and almost anything imaginable was bought and sold. Sadly that included Africans from time to time. Other than that Jacob was enthralled by The Plaine, and the many acquaintances that became names and stories that filled the notebooks he would bring back to Amsterdam.

Jacob frequently met Catalina Trico in New Amsterdam's "town square." Catalina was one of the very first settlers here coming to New Netherlands at 18 in 1624, newly married to Joris Rapalje. Now 48 when Jacob met her she had borne 11 children. She and her family lived on Pearl Street not far at all from the fort. Catalina was always the center of activity whenever she appeared on The Plaine. She and Jacob grew fond of each other in the brief time Jacob had been visiting New Amsterdam. Catalina had more tales and stories about New Amsterdam than anyone. She had been there since the beginning and seen it all. Thanks to Catalina Jacob's notebooks had a richness that they would otherwise have lacked.

Jacob was convinced more than anything by what he saw and heard on The Plaine that Jewish settlers would be right at home here in spite of the presence of Old Stuyvesant and those who thought like him. This was a marketplace where Jews could do business and contribute to the young city and make a mark for themselves.

Chapter 5

Then it was the morning of September 7, 1654, the day Jacob Barsimson would never forget. While he was standing in the middle of The Plaine gazing at the huge harbor, in the distance he saw a glimmer of white grow larger and larger. He soon realized it was an arriving ship. The only question on his mind was it headed toward or coming from Europe. The answer would change his life and Jewish life forever in America.

New Amsterdam's harbor was and is wide and deep. For Jacob mesmerized by the ship in the distance moving ever closer the harbor sparkled in the sun a deep shade of blue, small ripples punctuating the surface. Along the shorelines on both sides were luscious green forests that gave way to expansive meadows that gave way to rollicking hills in this newly found wonderland.

As for the mysterious ship the riveting focus of Jacob's attention as the harbor and shore faded away in his mind's eye, the ship appeared aglow with bolts of light shooting from its deck as the sun caught the surface of its cannons and ornamental metal work provided this golden orb riding ever higher in the sky became mirrors to reflect its celestial glory as it approached the shore.

The moment seemed to last forever then in what seemed an instant the ship was practically touching the shore where Jacob stood having come to a halt near the water's edge as he watched its anchor reach below the surface to bury itself in the harbor's rich underbelly. Jacob Barsimson so entranced by this ship's grand approach to New Amsterdam, did not even realize he had traversed The Plaine and literally walked into harbor if only a step or two but far enough to soak his shoes before he realized what he had done.

Jacob Barsimson's amazement was about to reach far higher. On the deck he could now clearly see a group of individuals young and older, men and women who he could identify better than any of those who now crowded the shore to greet the arriving ship. To Jacob's utter disbelief there were fellow Jews. Quite a few

and they were about to come on shore. What a

moment it was !

Chapter 6

Suddenly in a flash of light everything changed. It was night. It was cold. Jacob was back standing in a park in the present not hundreds of years ago on what seemed a stage, surrounded by many thousands of adults and children. All dressed very differently than him. Indeed strangely dressed. They were all unrecognizable.

Then he turned around to see more familiar faces and Asser Levy walking toward him. His booming voice reached out. Overpowering him " Jacob welcome back. You seemed in a trance and I knew you and your mind were back to

September 7, 1654, that glorious day we will never forget weren't you."

"Well I remember it as well as you do, so do all of us," Asser said to Jacob as he gazed toward the other 22 men, women, and children, up on the stage in the middle of the park snow gently falling down upon them. The icy flakes clinging to their clothes and the light of the full moon making them twinkle like diamonds.

At that point once again they all broke into dance and song gliding around the stage in great circles. Joining hands then separating then joining again singing Jewish songs with the voices of Angels.

Once they stopped Asser said to Jacob, " shall I tell the story of our landing HERE this time. If you remember you did last year Jacob." Yes yes I remember now go ahead Asser unless you make mistakes then I'll speak up and correct you."

Asser looked all around the park making contact with everyone's eyes thousands of eyes. Bowling Green Park was packed with many more still outside the historic fence that enclosed it. It was the First Night of Chanukah once again !

Asser began to speak. " Once he climbed down the rope ladder over the side of St. Catherine, the ship that brought him and his congregation of men, women and children all fleeing Portuguese Brazil tired and weary more to the point we were exhausted and dispirited from having left our home in Recife on the east coast of Brazil as we were in danger for our lives."

" Now we were refugees from oppression there in Brazil that forced us to flee. Some of our brothers and sisters were not as lucky as us, slaughtered by the Portuguese driving the Dutch out of Brazil and all the Jews most of all."

" So here we are on the afternoon of September 7, 1654, all members of the same Congregation in Recife, now making our way to shore in a distant foreign land walking through the shallow water lapping the shore not knowing what to expect or what to find in this new land. The sea did not part for us ! "

Right about there pointing beyond the fence here in present day Bowling Green so many years later, long ago stood Jacob once again looking at Asser back then and saying to him,

"I will never forget the look of surprise and joy on his face as we came close enough to shore that he had no doubt we were Jews just like him. When I came within a few feet of him yes I will never forget Jacob's words. "What I don't believe this."

" I introduced him to my wife, children and the others and explained our plight. Since the ship would not be leaving for a few days after taking on supplies and beaver pelts from the trappers here, Jacob found us a place to stay and explained why he was here and his plans to return to Amsterdam on the very ship the one that brought us here."

" It did not take long for Jacob to tell us about the wonders of this New World and the report he would make to Jewish leaders back in Amsterdam, that New Amsterdam held good prospects for Jewish settlers to live and prosper here."

" We quickly talked among ourselves and decided to stay here, try again to live in a new world and not go back to Europe. It did not take much urging for Jacob to decide to do the same and join us as a community of Jews in New Amsterdam. Rather than present his report in person Jacob carefully bundled and sealed his many notes and gave them to the captain of the Saint Catherine with instructions to deliver them once he arrived in Amsterdam."

Then it happened again. There was an unearthly blinding flash of white light and they were all back in New Amsterdam, September 1654. All of them including the large crowd from the present who had gathered to witness this Miracle. Now everyone was standing on this flat sandy plain. All the tall buildings shining with light from their windows had disappeared. The park was gone. Looming over them like some ancient forbidding walled fortress was Fort Amsterdam with the harbor now only yards away from its imposing large dark doors. Everyone up on the stage which did not disappear, seemed very concerned most of all Asser and Jacob. They knew only too well what took place there.

Yes the fort the dark brooding fort even now it seemed larger in their minds than it was originally. But its size was not the issue. The power that resided inside was. It was the enclosure where the ultimate power still lived in this young colony now a town a small city. While the colonists had won their freedom as an independent city with a charter of self-government the year before in 1653, it did nothing to change who controlled the soldiers and the guns, and the store of precious items the new city needed to survive.

Most of all living and ruling inside Fort Amsterdam was the figure everyone feared the most, free colony or not. And none more than these Jews who had just arrived as they would all soon learn from Jacob Barsimson and then for themselves.

So now being transported somehow back back all the way back to their arrival in 1654 they felt the terror again. Indeed they had no way of knowing if they were in some kind of trance or was it truly 1654 again. And it didn't make any difference anyway. They felt the terror once more that Peter Stuyvesant represented.

Here they were. Then they began to leave the stage all 24 of them these Jewish men, women and children plus Jacob drawn to the front of the fort like some dreadful magnet pulling at their souls. Asser and Jacob led the way.

They stood there huddled together directly facing those sinister black doors with handles shaped like hungry lions only making them more repelling. Everyone else this 21st century crowd gathered at Bowling Green who had come to celebrate Chanukah remained behind circling the stage and far beyond, their numbers were so large all of them glued to the drama taking place in front of the fort mesmerized by the trance they were experiencing.

" It's time Asser we might as well go in we can't avoid him." He was as everyone knew the one legged frightful Director General Peter Stuyvesant. Jacob had explained all about Stuyvesant right after the 23 landed and his own encounter only weeks earlier. Not that they would not have known soon enough even if Jacob had never been here to greet them as anyone landing in Stuyvesant's town did. First thing you must do present yourself to the Director General.

It may not have been as Inquisition the terror of torture and death and destruction which had greeted Jews so many other places through-out history. But the feeling about to go through those doors into Stuyvesant's den to gain accep-tance or rejection felt much the same. They knew fear but displayed courage.

Having walked the dirt and few cobblestoned streets of New Amsterdam, Jacob who knew every foot of this tiny town after his inquisitive two weeks spent here before Asser Levy and the others arrived and meeting the eclectic range of about 2000 inhabitants from all over Earth who spoke 18 different languages what an amazing place – that moment with Asser Levy's enthusi-asm and encouragement all 23 agreed they did not need to wander further. They would make New Amsterdam their new home.

Now they could not delay any longer appearing before Stuyvesant without his soldiers rounding them all up and putting them back on the ship in chains. So Asser and Jacob banged hard on the doors and they were opened from within.

" We are here to see the Director General. We have just arrived." To which the guard replied in a nasty tone his searing eyes slowly investigating them from the bottom of their shoes to the top of their hats. Then he eyed all the others standing near them. " What are you Jews. We never see Jews here except for this one," pointing at Jacob. " I had no idea there were more of you. Old Man Stuyvesant he's gonna start cursing seeing so many Jews here."

With that the ill clad menacing guard who limped like Stuyvesant but had both his legs led Jacob and Asser inside the fort while he warned the others to stay where they were not go wandering around. He told them " two of you inside the fort is enough no more or I'll get a beating from Old Pegleg."

The fort was quite large like a mini-city. His first time here Jacob barely noticed all the activity. There was a chapel, the governor's house, officers' lodging, and another structure a barracks for foot soldiers. There was a large well for drawing water, a sally port a separate entrance for the troops to use, a kitchen to feed all of those housed in the fort, two outhouses, a structure for keeping armaments and munitions, and a stable for horses. But it was only the gover-nor's house where Stuyvesant spent his days that meant anything to them. It was the heart of darkness for them.

While they stood outside and waited the guard disappeared inside. Then as he quickly rushed out and back to his post. He nervously told them he is coming out. Having two Jews inside was more than Old Peter Stuyvesant could bear.

Jacob and Asser heard him before they saw Stuyvesant. The rhythmic tapping of his wooden peg leg against the floor within. Then he emerged. Very imposing physically and the scowl on his face was very noticeable, and his small dark eyes. He was dressed like someone who knew or thought he was important with his fancy long coat, over sized breast belt and fur lined hat festooned with fancy pins and buttons.

Stuyvesant locked his small dark eyes on Jacob Barsimson.

" What are you still doing here." Before Jacob could answer Stuyvesant turned his evil gaze on Asser, and in a tone of disgust barked out, " And who is this Jew why is he here."

What followed was not a pleasant discussion. It was an interrogation. Jacob and Asser explained their interest in staying in New Amsterdam. Making new lives here with the others who arrived with them. After the shock wore off his face Stuyvesant let them know in no uncertain terms why that would not be a good idea. He alternated between trying to scare them and offering friendly advice why they would be better off elsewhere. Any where else but here. " The last thing we need are Jews," he growled.

Asser and Jacob most of all noticed Stuyvesant was a little less belligerent than he could have been or his mean reputation might have led them to expect. They knew why. Some recent good fortune made him less of a dictator. Now that this town recently became somewhat free of him with its own government which elected officials and judges, it was no longer his to rule with absolute control as though he was a king here with unlimited power.

Yet there was something far more significant that had Stuyvesant addressing them less forcefully than they knew was on his mind they being

Jews. As Jews Jacob Barsimson knew of course and had told Asser Levy that there were wealthy successful Jewish merchants back in Europe in Amsterdam who were investors in the Dutch West India Company, Stuyvesant's employer.

Stuyvesant had made a very nice life for himself in New Amsterdam and the idea of losing this assignment bothered him even far more than the Jews who he despised facing him that afternoon. Even though there was no doubt he wanted them gone and would surely write back to Amsterdam to make his case these Jews should be told to leave. So Stuyvesant was a little cautious for the moment

After this mostly one sided discussion which seemed to go on and on with Jacob and Asser saying little, finally Stuyvesant stood there silently for what seemed like hours but was only minutes, then he spoke again. "I will not give you permission to settle here and live your Jewish way of life in our God fearing Christian community but you do not have to get back on the St. Catherine and sail away on her tomorrow. I will wait for the next ship to arrive to take you some place else where Jews can be with their own."

What Stuyvesant was doing was buying time since he did not know if chasing away these Jews might cause him problems. Then came the warning he practically shouted at them, " I do not want you mingling with the others here anymore than is absolutely necessary. I don't want you or your children spending time on The Plaine or the market in front of the fort."

Stuyvesant concluded this meeting by walking right up to them only inches away his peg leg pounding the ground, " Most of all do not dare practice your ungodly rituals your so called religion anywhere in New Amsterdam. If you do I'll have all of you chained to the wall of the fort until the next ship comes to take you away."

With that Stuyvesant abruptly pivoted on his wooden leg and quickly was gone back inside. Right away Asser and Jacob realized the guard had reappeared pointing a musket at them and hurried them out of the fort. The doors slammed loudly behind them as they greeted the other 22 Jews standing outside exactly where they had left them what seemed like an eternity ago

worried about Asser and Jacob in the fort alone.

Chapter 7

Jacob spoke " quickly there is no time to waste. We must draft a new letter to give to the Captain of the St. Catherine to take back with him when his ship leaves tomorrow." To give to the Jewish investors in the Dutch West India Company back in Amsterdam asking for their assistance so they could stay in New Amsterdam and telling them of their encounter with Stuyvesant. With that all 24 quickly departed The Plaine which stood in front of the fort.

As they slipped into the gathering darkness as the sun set over New Amsterdam, it happened again the great flash of light and they were magically transported back to the present here in the 21st century making their way through the crowd back onto the stage and all around them the tall buildings and glowing lights reaching into the sky all around them witnesses to what was taking place.

Everyone ran back into the center of the park 24 figures men, women and children, then Asser spoke to the very large crowd that kept growing bigger, " So now you know. Being there in your imagination with us back in 1654. Transported through time more than 350 years ago. This magical force that has brought us all together today. Is it G-d. Or some other benevolent power none of us can comprehend or understand. We do not know but we are thankful. Reliving these powerful historic moments again and again each Chanukah and more and more of you able to experience our journey as the First Jews in America as your own."

At that point Jacob spoke up. " So now that we are back in the present let me tell all of you what happened after our encounter with Peter Stuyvesant when we left the fort. Right there pointing again to the area that is now right in front of the Custom House. "We told everyone who had waited for us so so eagerly while kneeling and standing as if holding a vigil, we told them what had happened all of it and most of all YES we would be staying for now anyway. Then we quickly left for our temporary lodgings close by on Beaver Street. There was work to be done."

It was Asser Levy who continued, " And so we did " he told the crowd with his booming voice. " And the next day we watched the St. Catherine sail out of the harbor until it was nothing more than speck of white from its sails as it disappeared on these azure waters and tucked with the Captain's papers in his cabin our letter we wrote the night before after leaving the fort that would decide our fate. That is as we prayed and prayed the ship would arrive safely crossing the Atlantic Ocean during hurricane season."

For the first time one of the women in the group wearing her traditional Jewish attire came closer and stood by Asser's side and spoke.

"After that we went about our lives and raising our children always aware that Stuyvesant's men were watching us looking for any reason to carry out his threat to chain us all to the fort and expel us from the colony as soon as the next ship arrived."

" We were extra careful on the Sabbath a regular day of work and commerce for everyone else except we 24 Jews. We did not intend to allow old Stuyvesant's threats to keep us from our Sabbath services or the High Holy Days fast approaching but we knew we needed to be very discreet. So as we read the Torah, sang our hymns, offered our sacrifices, and prayed to G-d in our temporary homes we kept the windows covered and a few of the men made the ultimate sacrifice for our greater good and stayed outside working to divert attention and camouflage our activities from Peter Stuyvesant's spies lurking all around us all the time."

Jacob now spoke again, "That is how we spent the fall of 1654 and making ourselves useful setting up small temporary shops and trading with the others who lived in New Amsterdam, as the cold winter crept up on us while we were working, praying, teaching our children and quietly building good relations in the town, thinking about businesses we might start if we were able to stay and live our lives here, and most of all avoiding Stuyvesant, staying away from his fort. We knew we would not possibly hear anything from Amsterdam in reply to our letter at least until the spring so we prepared ourselves for our first winter here."

Again that unearthly flash of light and it is 1654 once more. This time nighttime in December, a cold wind blowing from the harbor, and the area in front of the fort desolate except for 24 figures huddled against the cold and carrying something. As the snow begins to fall and coat the fort white making it look more inviting than it really was, as though it might be a grand welcoming palace where Jews could celebrate the First Night of Chanukah ever in New Amsterdam or anywhere else in North America.

They knew even if no one else did or cared here in December 1654 for the first time in human history Jews were celebrating the First Night of Chanukah in this New World although it was not much of a celebration. It is why Asser Levy,

Jacob Barsimson and all the other members of their small community down to the youngest child had gathered this cold evening at sunset in New Amsterdam on The Plaine in front of the fort while everyone else was in their tiny homes up and down Broadway and the surrounding streets gathered around their fireplaces keeping warm having no idea it was Chanukah or what Chanukah was.

Chapter 8

It was Saturday evening just after Sabbath, December 5, 1654. Remember the date and never ever forget it.

It was an outrageous idea but they were sick and tired of being Jews behind closed doors to keep Stuyvesant from persecuting them even more. It would be an act of defiance just like the Maccabees over 2000 years ago defied the Greek Syrians, defeated them, recaptured, and rededicated the Temple and then kept the Temple Menorah lighted for 8 days and nights with lamp oil enough for only one day. It was a miracle and an omen and it became the festival of Chanukah celebrated from that time forward by Jews across the world. Chanukah was and is and will always be a powerful symbol for Jews of persisting no matter the odds and good overcoming evil to bring light to the world. It is a Jewish story everyone should embrace as a valuable lesson.

Now for the first time in this New World, Asser and Jacob hatched the idea to be as courageous as their Maccabee ancestors and bring Chanukiah right to the very center of New Amsterdam, the very place in front of the fort where during daytime year round it was the most active place in all of New Amsterdam with markets and festivals, people meeting and children playing. And the place where Peter Stuyvesant's soldiers frequently marched as a clear sign of his power in this small growing new city.

They had carried with them all the way from Recife, Brazil, as they fled their most cherished possessions their Torah, their Sabbath clothing and small, handcrafted golden Menorah. Now for the first time they carried it to The Plaine this First Night of Chanukah. The snow had stopped, the sky cleared and a full bright Moon provided a heavenly glow that warmed their souls if nothing else bundled against the fierce winter cold and the wind from the harbor.

They made a circle, men, women, and children all 24 of them with their Menorah in the center as they protected it from the wind. They said prayers, sang hymns, read from the Bible, and finally the glorious moment. Asser had carried a small lantern with them. He took a wick from his pocket and drew flame from the lantern. Then he held the flame in his hands and passed it one to the other each face illuminated with a look of joy until it passed through all 24 pairs of hands returning where it began in Asser Levy's hands.

Then he said to all of them, " let us do this tonight light the candles for ourselves and for all Jews who will follow us to this New World for generations to come for hundreds of years until the end of Time. May what we do tonight Light the Way for all of them. We will most likely be long forgotten in the mist of Time but may our

Spirits remain within this Circle to return to this place in the future."

"May Chanukah be celebrated by Jews here forever more."

As those gathered in the park and beyond the park these hundreds of years later transported in Time back to December 1654, experienced all this as much as these 24 Jews had back in 1654 where Bowling Green is today. It was truly magical for all of them.

Asser and Jacob had made a decision while this was the First Night of Chanukah in their New World and they should only have lighted the center candle and the first of 8 candles, with four on each side of their small Menorah, they decided to light all the candles to make sure everyone watching this strange sight from the windows of their small homes surrounding The Plaine, and Stuyvesant's soldiers watching from the fort, they would all see these Jews openly celebrating their religion and their traditions.

After lighting all the candles they formed a procession and walked up Broadway, led by Asser and Jacob carrying their Menorah which miraculously remined lighted all the candles as a howling wind filled the streets. They walked up to the wall now Wall Street turned right and then right again onto Broad Street, to their lodgings near Beaver Street. They wanted everyone who lived in New Amsterdam to see that they were shining their light on this New World there and heavenly light brightened all of New Amsterdam that night.

All those gathered in and around the park today transported in their minds back in Time experienced all this every bit as much as Asser and this tribe of Jews inspired to form a new Congregation not long after this First Chanukah, named Shearith Israel.

The gathered crowd living in the 21st century standing at Bowling Green understood all this in ways they could not logically comprehend as though each of them had been one of these first 24 Jews to arrive here. They saw it in their mind's eye.

Then suddenly they were back in our time, and in the middle of the park appeared as larger than life a simple but elegant gold colored Menorah. For now was the most special moment of all when the Spirits of Asser, Jacob and 22 other original Jewish settlers would continue the tradition begun back in 1654 renewed every year at Chanukah famous all over the world for this miracle of Chanukah.

For right now there was much singing and dancing on the stage and throughout the large crowd which had gathered to witness this annual miracle. Music and dance emerging from thousands of years of Jewish life, religion, and tradition. It all seemed so new again. It went on and on as darkness fell over Bowling Green and the sun glided away behind the Statue of Liberty in the harbor to rest for the night. What a night it was and will be again and again !

Then it was time to Light the Menorah and all this celebrating as it is every year would be repeated again tomorrow and for all the 8 nights of Chanukah. As he had for the first time back in 1654 right here so long ago, Asser motioned to Jacob, and the large ornamental rod Jacob had with him when he first appeared it turned into a bright flaming torch as Jacob stood before the glowing Menorah and lighted the world with the spirit of Chanukah as the entire park and the thousands upon thousands in it and beyond were bathed in an unearthly magical light they could grab in their hands and pass it one to another as it turned into the colors of the rainbow as the singing and dancing again engulfed everyone in pure joy and goodwill for everyone to see and hear.

And so this is the story of the First Jews to come to and settle in North America and the first Chanukah in December 1654 at a place where much American history would be made for generations to come, where Chanukah became destined to be celebrated for all time here at Bowling Green, where Jacob Barsimson, Asser Levy and 22 other Jewish men, women and children began the Jewish experience in America that will never end.

One more mystery. Why did the Spirits of these 24 after they had all died return back here for the first time again for Chanukah in 1776 and every year since ? Because it was in July 1776 New Amsterdam by then New York City was liberated from oppression and freedom rang out across the city and new nation. Right here at Bowling Green where they had celebrated their first Chanukah in 1654 and lighted their Menorah is the place where the hated statue of the King of England stood from 1770 until the night of July 9, 1776, when the residents of the city proclaimed their freedom from oppression by destroying the statue of the hated King.

That powerful event resonated throughout the land and the ages and awakened the Spirits of those first 24 Jews, sent them a cosmic signal to return here again and again each Chanukah to participate as Jews in this burst of freedom for an America where all can celebrate their own religions. Jews and non-Jews alike.

No no no this is not the end of this story.

Read on the best is yet to come !

Because then the ultimate Truth was revealed for all to see. All of these 24 Jewish pioneers, trail blazers, were transformed and became far more radiant for all to see. These 24 were indeed Angels of G-D. The one called Asser then spoke to all as only Angels are allowed to say His name ... "All Glory to God as we all of us are His children."

To everyone's surprise even though this celebration took place every year these 24 men, women and children, these Spirits of the First Jews in America, these Angels began to take on a different form. They were transformed into Jews famous Jews, important Jews, and forgotten Jews who should be remembered all who made a difference here in America for more than 350 years now. The crowd grew silent again and all eyes drawn to the center of the park.

A display of pure splendor was now underway. A transformation.

The "night of nights" as it has come to be known and appreciated by the thousands upon thousands of Jews and non-Jews drawn to Bowling Green Park every Chanukah for 8 nights, and millions more around the world who have all learned about Chanukah at Bowling Green, it is best know for the spectacular "grand finale" that concludes each night's celebration when these

24 Spirits come alive, call them what they are Angels of G-D begin their heavenly super-natural tribute to Jews throughout our history.

Up on the wonderful and perfect circular stage surrounding the Bowling Green Menorah these 24 turn themselves into an unfolding cavalcade of Jews in America who have followed the original 24 and who have made a mark as Jews in America. This ultimate tribute to American Jews changes year after year with an ever revolving collection of Jewish women and men being honored in this magical way.

Momentarily coming to life again for those assembled to see them as they were in life in their prime. Nothing is said, nothing needs to be said, the assembled crowd simply beyond explanation know in their minds who each individual who metamorphoses before them on stage is and was in life and what they accomplished that makes each of them so special. Indeed some not many of the Jews honored by the Angels are alive today if not physically present that evening.

And so it was this First Night of Chanukah the grand finale that those who witnessed it would never forget as long as they lived. It was an experience that transformed everyone's life and the Jews who witnessed this miracle at Bowling Green were always inspired to live their lives in ways that one day they might as a result of their good deeds while they lived they too might one day forever be honored in this way by the Angels of 1654 !

Each night of Chanukah this glorious event ends with Psalm 150 as sung by the Angels every-one has come to know as Asser Levy. Sung so beautifully each person in the crowd is either stunned, crying for joy, or literally transported out of their bodies and merge their souls with everyone else there.

Then it was over. With a final burst of song and dance these 24 timeless figures in the center of the park up on stage returned to their original form appearing again as they looked more than 350 years ago back in 1654, standing in front of the infamous fort at New Amsterdam. As silence descended on the park all those who had gathered that evening departed for their homes and all the far flung corners of the Globe. Their lives changed forever.

Jews understood as they had never before the meaning of their unique role in human history, and their many responsibilities to their religion and to other Jews and most of all to all Beings of goodwill who walked the Earth. Their story for everyone.

All the many non-Jews who had likewise flooded into Bowling Green this night and all the others to see and experience for themselves, understood as they had never before why Jews are God's Chosen People, chosen by God to teach all the world's people how a community determined to survive and prosper built upon its shared religion, united by bonds of Belief that reach into their Souls, will not allow any Evil they have suffered or any challenges to destroy what they have created with the Blessing of and under the watchful eyes of G-D.

When all had departed silence again reigned at Bowling Green, all that remained was the glowing Menorah in the center of the park and upon the stage only Jacob Barsimson and Asser Levy, as the Angels who they are. Nothing needed to be said for they both knew all that needed to be known as they always had and always would. As the walked arm in arm to and fro on this Heavenly stage alone.

Then something happened that had never happened before. Simultaneously Jacob and

Asser noticed a dark figure at the edge of the park coming from what seemed inside the Custom House where Fort Amsterdam had stood. As the figure moved hesitantly closer neither now had any doubt. The sound of each step was something neither would ever forget. It was Peter Stuyvesant more accurately his Spirit approaching them.

Then he was up on the stage.

Two good Spirits and one evil Spirit face to face as they had been way back in September 1654. An even deeper silence now filled the cold air. Then Stuyvesant's spirit spoke to them. " I have now spent hundreds of years roaming the shadows, deprived of sleep or the peace the grave should have brought me. I am punished for my sins against you."

Stuyvesant continued, " My intolerance in life, my hatred for those I deemed different than me, and worst of all my treatment of Jews who came to New Amsterdam seeking a new life are my punishment. You two and all those who came with you deserved far better from me."

The two Angels put their hands on his shoulders and said, " In the name of He who sent us you are forgiven now that you understand what you did so long ago and seek our forgiveness. These last 350 years and more are punishment enough as long as we never forget what happened here. What you did. Go now rest in peace for eternity. With that Stuyvesant disappeared from this Earth forever.

This is the story of the past, present and future of the First Chanukah in America. It took place at Bowling Green and always will just as it has been recounted here. Except for what took place in December 2020. It got better much better !

The Spirits of Jacob and Asser and the others decided they should remain in Bowling Green year round every day and night in a symbolic way. They transformed themselves into a Circle of Light, 24 candles in the middle of the park surrounding the fountain to come alive as blazing torches every night of the year after sunset.

They would always come alive in person each Chanukah for 8 nights at Bowling Green to please the ever larger crowds that gather here at Chanukah, but from now on these 24 Jews will always be here every day and night in Bowling Green.

A Circle of Light to illuminate the world and make it a better place.

END OF STORY

BEGINNING OF JEWISH
EXPERIENCE IN AMERICA

PART TWO

Background information

about the First Jews, Chanukah

& History of Bowling Green

Introduction

Bowling Green's history

Celebrating Chanukah @ Bowling Green

Bowling Green Center of a Universe

Tribute to the First Jews

INTRODUCTION – PART TWO

It is now the 288th anniversary of the creation of Bowling Green, the oldest public park in America, and 33rd anniversary of the Bowling Green Association taking place here in early Fall 2021.

My interest in Bowling Green began back in 1983, when I was working for a company on Whitehall Street and like many others in the spring and summer I would sit in Bowling Green at lunchtime. Unlike many of the others filling the benches I was curious about and interested in the park itself and became fascinating on learning it was the oldest park in New York City. Only later that it is the oldest public park in America.

Now almost 40 years later since first "discovering" Bowling Green much has changed and much remains the same. As with everything there is a lesson here or more to the point lessons. Back then I became disappointed with the lack of attention Bowling Green received from NYC government and likewise the one dominant organization here back in the 1980s, the Downtown-Lower Manhattan Association.

I remain disappointed by the lack of attention Bowling Green receives from NYC government and the dominant group here now the Alliance for Downtown New York ironically created by the Downtown - Lower Manhattan Association which exists today tucked into the structure of the Alliance for Downtown New York.

This "microcosm" Bowling Green and the surrounding community reflects larger issues as it should as one of the most notable places in America and American history. There have been five New York City Mayors since I became interested in Bowling Green, Ed Koch, David Dinkins, Rudy Giuliani, Michael Bloomberg, and Bill de Blasio. As close as Bowling Green is to City Hall and even though New York City was created here in 1653, in these 38 years not one of them has ever come to Bowling Green to celebrate its history or its importance.

They were each at Bowling Green for only one reason because ticker tape parades begin here and paying no attention to Bowling Green itself. Dinkins, Bloomberg, and de Blasio were each here one other time for a reason having nothing to do with Bowling Green itself. That is it.

Meaningful in a symbolic way because it reflects their attitudes toward the city and this place. There is no specific political value for them in identifying with or giving attention to Bowling Green and so they and their administrations and other like minded groups do not.

In this community as in others around the nation too many give too little attention to very local issues and places and we all suffer as a result. There are a few enlightened individuals and organizations and companies that care but too many do not. Here in Lower Manhattan which traditionally has been a business district and still is even as the residential character of the area has developed – most companies and their executives do not identify with the community in which they do business.

Bowling Green as an example means nothing to them. Very few have a clue about the history or value of the park or the area. This lack of local community participation by many is corrosive. At least some care.

So what has changed at and around Bowling Green which I am proud of and that reflects how any of us can make a local difference in the face of disinterest among those with power and funds. First of all, progress is possible not as much as I would like but to an extent working around the problem if you are not intimidated by being ignored and even mocked.

Bowling Green was often dirty when I first arrived. The Park was not being cleaned regularly. In that case simply having someone like myself knowing how to effectively complain did force the Parks Dept. to pay attention to this basic issue as long as I kept reminding them.

I also became interested in the fact there was no Christmas Tree each December in our oldest park in so prominent a location. City Hall and the Parks Dept. was not persuaded by my requests except to tell me if I was able to raise the necessary funds they would allow me to erect a Christmas Tree and lights in Bowling Green which I did after some effort for the first time in December 1986, and for 18 more years after, larger and larger Trees some the size of Rockefeller Center and at Bowling Green in 2004 the first public Christmas Tree ever illuminated anywhere with LEDs.

Another notable Bowling Green Christmas Tree was December 2001, following the terror attacks at the World Trade Center. Large amounts of gold and silver bars were stored in a hardened vault deep in the basement of one of the Towers. In November 2001, the vault was uncovered and the gold and silver recovered. I was able to convince the Bank of Nova Scotia responsible for this gold and silver to donate bars of this 9/11 silver to the Bowling Green Association so we could create large pure silver Angels ornaments for the Christmas Tree almost 400 Angels one for each of the Fire Fighters and Police Officers killed on 9/11, each engraved with one name and after the Christmas Tree came down each of the Angels was specially boxed and sent to their families.

The first two Trees 1986 and 1987 prior to the formation of the Bowling Green Association, as a result was created to do more year round at Bowling Green and in Lower Manhattan filling a void in this community.

Here is a pointed example of how poorly Bowling Green Park is treated by City Hall and the Parks Dept. I learned the wrought iron fence that surrounds Bowling Green is a National Historic Landmark because of the famous Revolutionary War event that took place here on July 9, 1776, when New York colonists celebrating Independence smashed through this locked fence that had been installed by the British in 1771, and the colonist destroyed the statue of George III in the middle of the park.

In 1987 I saw how much the fence was in need of new paint and I told the Manhattan Commissioner of the NYC Park Dept.. He told me sorry we don't have anyone to paint the fence. So I decided to do it myself and asked him just for paint and brushes. Again sorry we don't have any to spare. So I spent weekends alone during 1987 giving this large fence two coats of paint under coat and primary buying the paint and brushes myself finishing in the winter just in time for the 1987 Christmas Tree Lighting.

As for lights there were also no permanent lights in Bowling Green. None at all complete darkness in the night for our oldest and most historic park and grand plaza. Again City Hall showed no interest so I found out who was in charge of lighting parks. It was the Dept. of Transportation not Parks, and a city official named Phil Brooks. I found his office in the Municipal Building went there, asked to see him and I made the case for Bowling Green. He agreed Bowling Green deserved to be illuminated and soon after eight powerful luminaires the same type as in Central Park and other parks were installed in Bowling Green for the first time.

Likewise, the U.S. Custom House at Bowling Green's exterior was completely dark at night. I was able to persuade the U.S. General Services Administrator for the New York region William Diamond, to install powerful floodlights to illuminate the U.S. Custom Hose after dark. Together the lights in Bowling Green and on the Custom House made a profound difference here at Bowling Green Plaza at night.

I promoted Bowling Green and its history vocally and year round organizing events throughout the year and lobbying for Lower Manhattan all the time. Through Bowling Green Association efforts, a second large flagpole was installed a gift of the Greek community. In December 1989 in a truly historic development I brought Arturo DiModica's 3 ½ ton larger than life bronze to Bowling Green and as a permanent gift here at no expense to New York City through Arturo DiModica's generosity.

Alexander Hamilton also ignored in Lower Manhattan became another project of the Bowling Green Association beginning in 1988 and with many many efforts in Hamilton's honor both at Bowling Green and in Trinity churchyard at Alexander Hamilton's grave. In 1992, I successfully had the U.S. Custom House at Bowling Green named for Hamilton.

1997 witnessed the first Menorah for Chanukah ever placed in Bowling Green Park accomplished by the Bowling Green Association in recognition of Bowling Green being where the First Jews to ever arrive in North America, in September 1654, and they settled right here.

So many flags have been raised here by nations from all over the world with the installation of the second flagpole in 1996. It allowed us to celebrate the origin of the St. Patrick's Day Parade here at Bowling Green back in 1762, raising the Irish flag here each St. Patrick's Day.

The Museum of American Finance, founded by John Herzog, had its origin at Bowling Green with two exhibits the first for Alexander Hamilton resulting from efforts of John Herzog and myself, the result of his interest in the Bowling Green Association.

The beginning and end of the American Revolution has been highlighted here as a result of the efforts of the Bowling Green Association among others and the north plaza co-named Evacuation Day Plaza by the NYC Council a few years ago.

I could detail so much more but I think this is enough here and now.

So what have I learned over these 30 plus years here at Bowling Green. What others have learned everywhere since the beginning of time that only power and money count and if you have neither no matter the cause it is always a battle whether at Bowling Green or anywhere else.

After nearly 40 years City Hall and the Parks Dept. pay no more attention to Bowling Green then they did back in 1983 and in some ways even less. The bright permanent lighting that was installed earlier has been removed and replaced by lights that do a poor job. The powerful floodlights that illuminated the U.S. Custom House no longer work. The walkway inside Bowling Green which was adequate was dug up only to be replaced with another dirt path that now floods with water whenever it rains.

City Hall refuses to illuminate Charging Bull the single most popular attraction in New York City so it stands in darkness at night even while many come here after dark to see and photograph Charging Bull. After Mayor Koch's decision to permit the placement of Charging Bull he and all four mayors who have followed him have ignored Charging Bull.

The annual Bowling Green Christmas Tree is no more as the cost of that ambitious project continued to increase and I could no longer raise the funds required for the tree, its installation and lighting. Once again we finally have a Christmas tree again but sadly a rather small tree.

Bowling Green from Charging Bull at its north plaza all the way to the Alexander Hamilton U.S. Custom House should be celebrated all year round and be inspiringly illuminated every night of the year. The large and impressive Bowling Green Christmas tree should glow again.

Instead the disregard both City Hall and the Alliance have for Bowling Green and its many values is a commentary on our society and our city.

So what is the message of Bowling Green I have learned over more than 30 years most of all it is still worth the effort no matter the odds or disappointments understanding how much better it should and can be.

THE RICH HISTORY OF BOWLING GREEN

For hundreds of years before the first Europeans arrived on Manhattan Island, Native American tribes in the region made use of Bowling Green as a ceremonial center and frequent entry point to New York harbor. Before landfill extended the island, the shoreline lapped at the edge of this plaza. In November 1613 Captain Adrian Block of the Netherlands set up winter camp just north from Bowling Green on Broadway when he became the first European to ever land on the island. On May 4, 1626, on behalf of the Dutch West India Co. Dutchman Peter Minuit formally established an outpost here at the tip of Manhattan Island and began construction of the first permanent structure Fort Amsterdam when he landed here at Bowling Green.

A few years later on June 2, 1635, the first Italian ever to set foot in North America Pietro Cesare Alberti age 27 from Venice landed here at what would become Bowling Green, settled here in New Amsterdam, married, and raised a large family, lived on Broad Street, and then went on to become a successful farmer in Brooklyn before Alberti and his wife were killed in an Indian raid in 1655. Many many other nationalities made their first arrival in this New World by coming to New Amsterdam just as Pietro Alberti did.

The small enclave grew with settlers arriving from all over the world. It is reported 18 different languages were spoken here back in the 1600s while the Dutch were in control. Then on February 2, 1653, a momentous event took place when after constant clamoring by the colonists to the Dutch West Indies Company in Holland, and all these settlers living south of what is now Wall Street – on February 2, 1653, the enclave officially became New Amsterdam and the first city and the first self-governing territory in North America when on that day the settlers were granted a charter by the Company and forming the Common Council (now the City Council) at a ceremony with

Director General Peter Stuyvesant within Fort Amsterdam which is today the site of the Alexander Hamilton U.S. Custom House.

The very first official act of the New Amsterdam Common Council took place on March 13, 1653, when they and Peter Stuyvesant agreed to begin construction of a wooden stockade a fence stretching from river to river to protect the new city from invasion. That is the wall that became Wall Street, a number of years later. Today the most famous street in the world.

The next momentous event at Bowling Green in Lower Manhattan was the arrival of the First Jews ever to set foot on North American soil. Arrived in September 1654. 23 men, women and children fleeing persecution in Brazil. After some initial resistance by Peter Stuyvesant, and with the support of investors in the Dutch West India Company back in Amsterdam they thrived here as a community, created the first Jewish Congregation in America, and built the first Synagogue on American soil nearby years later in 1730.

The British displaced the Dutch permanently September 8, 1664, and renamed the colony New York. Bowling Green remained New York's first town square until 1733, when at the urging of the New York colonists the plaza was officially named Bowling Green and made the first public park in North America, used for the sport of lawn bowling, on March 12, 1733.

The very first St. Patrick's Day Parade anywhere on Earth took place and began at Bowling Green on March 17, 1762. It was a simple march up and down Broadway both to celebrate Irish culture but also a defiant march against British rule both in Ireland and here in America.

On October 31, 1765, the march to American independence which would take place July 1776, had its beginnings at Bowling Green, where 11 Broadway stands today, the site of Burns Coffee House. Here 200 New York merchants, met and agreed to oppose the new British tax the Stamp Act, and sent word throughout the colonies urging others to do the same.

In 1770 after the repeal of the Stamp Act the British erected a gold leaded lead statue of King George III of England on horseback in the center of Bowling Green Park, and the following year built the now nationally landmarked fence much of which still stands, to protect the statue from the wrath of the freedom loving New York colonists.

On July 9, 1776, a copy of the Declaration of Independence arrived here from Philadelphia, and after being read on Broadway jubilant colonists ripped through the locked fence at Bowling Green and tore down the statue of George III in celebration as 133 British warships stood offshore.

Washington himself is claimed to have ridden down Broadway alone late that very evening on his white stallion, long after the colonists had left to walk in silence in the park among the shattered pieces of the statue of George III. In the following days the lead statue was melted down by the colonists, made into musket shot and the ammunition resulting used by George Washington's troops in the War for Independence.

At the end of the War on November 25, 1783, long known and famous as Evacuation Day, the last British troops on American soil left for home departing from Bowling Green, and the very last British flag flying anywhere in these United States was lowered and the American flag raised in the presence of General George Washington to formally end British occupation forever. The British had greased and tarred the flagpole at Bowling Green and embedded spikes in it to prevent the Union Jack from being taken down but a young New Yorker Thomas Van Arsdale climbed the pole tore off the British flag and replaced it with the Stars & Stripes. Bowling Green will always remain synonymous with the American flag.

In 1788 the ratification of the U.S. Constitution in New York was followed by a huge parade to Bowling Green in honor of Alexander Hamilton, its most influential and its pivotal supporter. The following year the new U.S. government was established with its first national capital in Lower Manhattan on Wall Street, and President Washington's second Official Mansion was just a few yards north of Bowling Green at 39 Broadway. Every one of the legendary American Founding Fathers could be found at one time or another enjoying their leisure in and around Bowling Green Park in the late 1700s.

And had the United States Capital stayed in New York City the original site which is now the Alexander Hamilton U.S. Custom House at Bowling Green, was in 1789 designated to become the official residence for U.S. Presidents in effect The White House. A mansion was built on the site that with the move of the U.S. capital south, became the official home of the New York State Governor until the state capital moved north to Albany.

The greatest New Yorker of all time Alexander Hamilton lived and practiced law for a number of years here at Bowling Green in a townhouse where 26 Broadway stands today. Many important and influential New Yorkers lived in homes surrounding Bowling Green in the years following the conclusion of the American Revolution and for years after.

In the years since Bowling Green has remained a public park and one of New York's best known plazas. 11 Broadway became the first notable high quality skyscrapers in New York City when it opened 125 years ago in 1896. Before moving uptown, 26 Broadway was the headquarters for John D. Rockefeller and his worldwide Standard Oil empire. And since the first ticker tape parade on October 29, 1896, every single one has begun here at Bowling Green.

Beginning in 1986, until recent years at the Holidays a very large Christmas tree had graced Bowling Green Park, second only to Rockefeller Center's in notoriety, and some years a larger tree than at Rockefeller Center, right here at Bowling Green. On December 20, 1989, what would become the most famous statue in New York, Arturo DiModica's 3 1/2 ton "Charging Bull" arrived at its current location. It is the most important gift of art ever made to New York City, and "Charging Bull" will remain where it is at Bowling Green forever the most visited attraction in this great city year after year.

And in March 1996, to celebrate the 175th anniversary of Greek Independence the Greek community in New York donated the second flagpole at Bowling Green. Bowling Green which has reigned as a symbol of freedom, independence and community spirit for generations continues to grow in stature as a sacred place in New York for nations and peoples from around the world to fly their national flags and celebrate each their own heritage their flag flying beside the original 13 star American flag .

In December 1997 for the first time ever a large Menorah was erected in the center of Bowling Green at Chanukah by the Bowling Green Association in honor of the first Jews ever to arrive in North America who did do here in September 1654. The fist Menorah was a towering 14 ft. work of sculpture created by the renowned sculptor of "Charging Bull" at Bowling Green, Arturo DiModica. Every year since a Menorah has been placed in the center of Bowling Green each Chanukah and always will. Most notably the first large public Menorah illuminated with LEDS was created for Bowling Green in December 2005 and has been used every Chanukah here since 2005.

Bowling Green is by far the most historic part of New York City as well as one of the most historic in the nation. Today Bowling Green is the most impressive plaza in New York City as it has long been and will remain.

CELEBRATING CHANUKAH @ BOWLING GREEN

There is no reason to believe nor evidence that a Menorah was ever placed in Bowling Green prior to December 1997. There is also no doubt the First Jews to arrive here in 1654 would have been found during that first Chanukah in North America December 1654 where Bowling Green stand today.

Once in 1997 I learned the story of these First Jews it became my goal that just as we had been erecting a very large Christmas Tree at Bowling Green since 1986, we must also begin erecting a Menorah in Bowling Green for Chanukah. I had no doubt the very best way to begin this new tradition.

I went to see by then my good friend the Italian American sculptor Arturo DiModica who I had convinced back in December 1989 to make a gift to Bowling Green of his new 3 ½ ton bronze sculpture, his larger than life "Charging Bull." It became an immediate phenomenon and by 1997 was legendary globally attracting millions of visitors every year.

I asked Arturo would he design and build a Menorah for Bowling Green as a work of original sculpture. Arturo did. He created a 14 ft. high Menorah of bronze with huge real light candles topped with copper covers. It was as stunning a Menorah as you will ever see and placed exactly in the center of the Bowling Green fountain. With its candles lighted and dancing inside their glass enclosures in the night sky it was an image I will never forget.

We only displayed Arturo's Menorah in Bowling Green that first Chanukah in December 1997. The story of what has happened with it since is a story all by itself but here is not the place for it. Without Arturo's Menorah in the years that followed I placed other uninspiring Menorahs in Bowling Green.

That is until December 2005. Allow me to introduce Philip Altheim one of the finest individuals I have ever met. Beginning in the mid-1990s Philip and the company he was president of Forest Electric played a pivotal role in the

Bowling Green Christmas tree. Philip donated all the electrical supplies and electricians needed to power and light these large Christmas trees often taller than 70 ft. each December. As Chanukah approached in December 2005 I expressed my frustration to the two Forest Electric electricians working on our Christmas tree as they had been year after year Tom Cummins and Andy Carson, telling them I did not have a special Menorah for Chanukah that was only a week away. To my complete surprise and without any request from me Tom Cummins said to me we can design and build you a new Menorah.

I replied to Tom you and Andy are two Irish American Catholic electricians and you are telling me you will design and build a new Menorah for Bowling Green and install it in time for Chanukah in one week ? Tom said yes as long as you get Philip Altheim to agree. Philip did without hesitating.

I had no idea what they would create or how but I made one prescient request. Beginning the year before we had started using LED Christmas lights on the Bowling Green tree, the first public Christmas tree ever to do so certainly here in the United States. I asked Tom and Andy please use these LED Christmas lights to illuminate the new Menorah. They agreed.

Once they called me a few days later from their workshop in the basement of One Rockefeller Center the building where the Rockefeller Center Christmas tree stands and back then still using old fashioned incandescent Christmas bulbs – Tom told me we are finished come see what we did.

I was stunned when I arrived and viewed their creation. It was simple elegant powerful and memorable. It was in its own way as impressive as Arturo DiModica's Menorah for Bowling Green back in 1997. It was their own design and made completely of off the shelf electrical components readily available in their workshop. I never expected what they accomplished.

Tom and Andy installed the Menorah in time for the First Night of Chanukah. It was and is the very first public Menorah ever illuminated with LED candles and we have erected it at Bowling Green every Chanukah since, and it is now officially named The Philip Altheim Menorah and always will be.

BOWLING GREEN CENTER
OF A UNIVERSE

Before we arrived long before

how long who knows

native peoples Indians

Columbus would call them

we did American Indians

who ruled Manhattan Island

the Iroquois nation

Manhattoes their name for their home

before Europeans

Explorer Henry Hudson

entered their giant harbor

teaming with sea life abundant

September 12, 1609

over 400 years ago

Hudson sailed his Half Moon

past our Bowling Green

keeping to the safety of their ship

first to land here Adriaen Block

in service to the Dutch

November 1613

while exploring this verdant island

his ship burned to its waterline where

World Trade Center would later stand

stranded with no hope of survival

Block and crew with nothing

only clothes they wore and little else

except for help of the local tribes

they built four huts on today's Broadway

then an Indian trail and spent

winter only yards north of

what would be Bowling Green

their epic story of survival

beginning November 1613

cooperation of Native Americans

7 years before Plymouth Rock

America's first Thanksgiving story

took place right here and in the Spring

Block built a new ship with their help the Onrust

sailed into Long Island Sound

named Block Island. For himself

(could have named Manhattan did not)

then returned to Europe and obscurity

here settlers who followed slowly

assembled southern tip Manhattan Island

now we call it Bowling Green

trappers traders farmers a polyglot

of nationalities many Dutch

all alone without direction

until May 4, 1626

Peter Minuit did arrive

sent by Dutch West Indies Company

rule the unruly bring order

build a fort plant the Dutch flag

here at what is Bowling Green

Fort Amsterdam first permanent structure

always creaky in disrepair

create the street pattern we walk today

area in from of fort later the Bowling Green

parade ground meeting place markets and more

New Amsterdam's town square

next a most important event Peter Stuyvesant arrives

rigid doctrinaire dictatorial Director General

absolute ruler till February 2, 1653

most historic date of all

new Charter written inside the fort

made New Amsterdam first self governing

place in all of the Americas

Common Council today's City Council

their first act to build the Wall

Mach 13, 1653

now most famous street on Earth

down at the Fort September 1654

among the new arrivals

23 Jews fleeing Brazil plus one more

stand before the Fort now Bowling Green

first Jews ever in North America

threatened by Peter Stuyvesant

go away from here !!

no they stayed and prospered

then comes 1664 England replaced the Dutch

New Amsterdam now New York

Fort Amsterdam now Fort James

Colony grew and grew until

colonists clamored to play their sport

on a manicured lawn bowling

where better than in front of the Fort !

they told the Council give us a park

so they did March 12, 1733

named it Bowling Green but

who would build it

John Chambers Peter Bayard Peter Jay

these 3 local businessmen did it

build the Green for them

how much did they get paid

one peppercorn a year for all three

to share and maintain the park

America's first public park !

for All to enjoy right up until today

next the spark of Revolution lit

where 11 Broadway stands today

more than 200 merchants met

Burn's Coffee House October 31, 1765

refuse Britain's Stamp Act sent their message

far and wide to other Colonies

New Yorkers converged on Bowling Green

Stamp Act Riots led to end of this tax

statue of King George III

erected in the center of Bowling Green

more protests followed a fence to protect the King

British build a fence and lock the park

a young boy arrives from St. Croix to make history

born on Nevis 1757 Alexander Hamilton

found his new American home

first visit to Bowling Green

soon to be Captain Hamilton

of the New York Militia

guarding cannons near Fort George

looking out on Bowling Green

surrounded still by a locked fence

until the Day of Days July 9, 1776

Word of Independence reaches here

defiant New Yorkers rip through the fence

destroy the statue of King George

first rebellious act of Revolutionary War

now it is official word spreads everywhere

the statue of the King is DEAD we are free

7 years later victory is won George Washington

comes here November 25, 1783, witness

last Union Jack lowered Stars & Stripes raised

here at Bowling Green call it Evacuation Day

Washington watches last British troops leave

more to come new Constitution drafted approved

1788 Alexander Hamilton hailed all over New York

parade down Broadway to Bowling Green

next first Capitol of nation New York City

April 30, 1789, Washington is President

September 11, 1789, Hamilton becomes

First Secretary of the Treasury

Savior of our new nation

mansion bult at Bowling Green

to be home for Presidents forever more

then Capitol is quickly gone first Philadelphia

next to Washington, DC

here at Bowling Green town houses successful merchants

Alexander Hamilton at 26 Broadway home and law office

Robert Fulton engineer designed his steamboat here

later still steamship companies on the Green

Cunard Line first among them

1907 brought impressive U.S. Custom House

today over a century later now

Alexander Hamilton U.S. Custom House

soon after Rockefeller came here

his Standard Oil Company to rule the world

same address as Hamilton 26 Broadway

(original Rockefeller Center)

through all this history and so much more

between the lines of these abridged verses

still Bowling Green Park remains

much as it was in March 1733

all but lawn bowling no more all was well or seemed to be

except never Christmas on the Green until 1986

towering Christmas Tree a joy for many years

at Bowling Green silent nights glowing lights

then O what a day December 20, 1989

our ultimate Christmas gift for ever more

Arturo DiModica's larger than life Charging Bull

what pandemonium what a surprise now

many millions visit every year always will

so much better than King George !

next to come was second 55 ft. flagpole

gift of the Greek Americans March 1996

another first Chanukah December 1997

where First Jews landed

Arturo DiModica's Menorah

Kamil Kubik's painting

made it famous !

as we create more history here

this story continues at Bowling Green

the epicenter of New York City

CIRCLE OF LIGHT

23 ways to change the world

messengers from Recife Brazil

found their way to this New World

there they build first synagogue

in South America

after fleeing for their lives

September 1654 brought them

north New Amsterdam

what is this place

will we stay ?

pioneers they found a way

built a Congregation

named it Shearith Israel

every step a struggle

equal rights for all their goal

every faith reaped their benefits

they began wrapped in poverty

followed by hostility and prejudice

governor sheriff reverend all

tried to block their path

Jews they fought back

thousands of years taught them well

struggle in their DNA

identity not denied

still prosper many generations gone by

New York and all across this land

back then a colony built on trade

Peter Minuet began that job later

notorious Peter Stuyvesant sent here

here to "greet" the arriving Jews

leave us alone go somewhere else

Stuyvesant huffed and puffed

venom from his mouth

fell on deaf Jewish ears

they heard it all long before

they would not let him get rid of them

this small town too good to leave

growing prosperous small city

18 languages they came

from everywhere

make their fortunes or

just survive in this New World

these Jews knew what to do

better still Dutch West India Company

it was their trading post

wealthy Jews back in Amsterdam

investors in this young company

these 23 Jews really 24 in all

made sure these investors

heard from them

they replied

Stuyvesant leave them alone !

Court records in this town

prove how adept they were

fighting for their rights

BurgoMasters & Schepens

powerful in New Amsterdam

gave these Jews their due in Court

these Jews call many Sephardim

some Ashkenazim too

they all arrived on a sailing ship

St. Catherine her name

arrived here September 7, 1654

pirates diverted them from their course

instead of Holland they landed here

Captain of the ship threw them off

so poor they could not pay their fares

soon they were in Court

battling for their rights

Asser Levy's name appears

he knew his way around the law

he was a leader for these pioneers

others prosecuted for working Sunday

day the rest of the colony prayed

Saturday just another workday

Sheriff Tienhoven tried locking

up Abraham De La Simon

sorry he failed too

Jews began to assert themselves

carefully for sure

back to Old Stuyvesant

reply he did not want from Amsterdam

date April 26, 1655, Dear Director General

leave these Jews alone we want them there !

they can live trade and travel as they please

Stuyvesant found other ways

keep these Jews at bay

we want to keep guard day or night

protect the colony like others do

petition of Jacob Barsimson

and Asser Levy DENIED !!

yes they fought back

they won the right !!

volunteer policemen they became

next a Jewish cemetery was their want

DENIED December 1655

APPROVED February 1656

being a Burgher was the highest honor

to be had in New Amsterdam

they held sway over everything

except evil Peter Stuyvesant

Asser Levy applied

denied then approved

Levy's leadership was legend

among New Amsterdam Jews

history notes Levy if not well enough

securing civil rights licenses permits

so much more equality for Jews

Levy stayed here longer than all the others

built a family stayed still when

British replaced Dutch

made this York City

prospered well

died here too

buried where no one knows

ashes some where under city streets

now all of them 23 plus one

LIVE in Bowling Green

forevermore for everyone

PART THREE

IMAGE
PORTFOLIO

View Bowling Green &

Chanukah @ Bowling Green

in a series of black & white images.

Take a tour like no other

& allow your imagination

to be your guide.

This is the most famous image in the history of Bowling Green,

a painting visualizing the night of July 9, 1776. When colonists

celebrated word of the Declaration of Independence reaching

New York City destroyed the hated statue of King George III

in middle of Bowling Green. It is the exact place where Jews

first stood in North America and where now stands the

Bowling Green Menorah each Chanukah.

Black and white image of colorful oil painted by Kamil Kubik

the night in December 1997 Chanukah first formally

celebrated in Bowling Green with the unveiling

of Arturo DiModica's new 14 ft. high

bronze Menorah with copper tops.

The very first Bowling Green Menorah in December 1997,

created by the great sculptor of "Charging Bull" Arturo Di Modica

at my request soon after I learned the First Jews to come here

to North America arrived right here. It was magnificent

work of sculpture 14 ft high in bronze with giant

real light candles with copper tops.

I tell the incredible fascinating story elsewhere of the current

Bowling Green Menorah the Philip Altheim Menorah created

and built December 2015 and used here ever since here.

These are the Irish American electricians Tom Cummins

and Andy Carson assembling this Menorah for

the first time in Bowling Green.

Tom Cummins inspecting LED lanterns for Bowling Green's

Menorah in December 2005 for their first use.

These were and are still the LED lights we used back

then on the large Bowling Green Christmas Tree.

This Menorah was the first public outdoor Menorah

anywhere on Earth illuminated with LED lights.

Andy Carson and Tom Cummins standing proudly

with the then new Bowling Green Menorah they created

and had just finished assembling for the first time

in Bowling Green in December 2005.

Viewing the Bowling Green Menorah in all its glory

in the middle of Bowling Green exactly where

the First Jews arrived September 1654.

The simplicity of the Bowling Green Menorah

is integral to the powerful impact it has.

While you cannot fully see it in this black & white photo

this Menorah constructed of golden looking parts

glows with dazzling brilliance during the day

when the sun shines directly on it.

A unique view of the Bowling Green Menorah at night

lights shining on it give it ethereal glow and

enhances its tremendous impact in

the middle of Bowling Green.

The Bowling Green Menorah each Chanukah stands in the

middle of Bowling Green and there it is centered on

Broadway between all the tall towers that

surround Bowling Green.

Here is the Bowling Green Menorah at sunset with

the harbor in the background and unseen but

visible standing there the Statue of Liberty.

Also in the foreground one of the 24 LED

Torches surrounding the Menorah

The Circle of Light

This is America's oldest public park designated March 12, 1733,

just one third acre far far more important and historic

than its small size seen here in winter.

Imagine this place in September 1654 before it was a park

back then known as The Plaine the flat sandy open space

in front of Fort Amsterdam the town's gathering place

see the first Jews standing in this New World here.

Winter's snow when it falls in December blankets

the Bowling Green Menorah adding mystery to its presence

It might have been snow like this that fell upon the first Jews

to arrive as they spent their First Chanukah

in New Amsterdam in 1654.

Another view the Bowling Green Menorah and

Bowling Green covered in snow in December

the Alexander Hamilton U.S. Custom House

its backdrop looking like it might be

a great Temple.

The Circle of Light in Bowling Green a wonderful tribute to the

first 24 Jews who arrived here September 1654 right now

in its first manifestation 24 solar powered torches

they come to life every night of the year.

A view of the stage surrounding Bowling Green's

Menorah just one year December 2007 another priceless

example of Philip Altheim's generosity one more reason

this is the Philip Altheim Menorah.

For the future a stage should be built here every Chanukah

just as in the story "Finding The Light" for 8 nights of

joyous celebration unlike anywhere in honor of

the First Chanukah in America right here !

Imagine Bowling Green's fountain turned into a stage surrounding

the Menorah each Chanukah as it was for the celebration of

the 10th anniversary of the First Menorah in Bowling Green

and as it is in the story "Finding the Light" and these

24 Jews who came right here in 1654 magically

come alive sing & dance as crowds fill

Bowling Green & far beyond for the Miracle

of Chanukah @ Bowling Green.

Ibrahim Kurtulus and others lighting the Bowling Green Menorah

December 19, 2017, the Alexander Hamilton U.S

Custom House behind them. This is an

image that captures the essence

of Chanukah.

Each December once Chanukah is over in the very same place

now each year a modest and beautiful Christmas tree

graces the center of the Bowling Green fountain

it is often left standing and lighted until

spring it becomes our Winter tree.

Bowling Green's Winter tree in February 2021 during the

pandemic stood tall and as vibrant during a winter snowstorm

as when installed for Christmas in December 2020.

The beauty of Bowling Green in snow

is impossible to deny I need no further

proof than what you see with

your own eyes.

Charging Bull is an overwhelming presence at Bowling Green

winter spring summer fall day and night since

December 20, 1989, and always will be.

The author at Bowling Green at Chanukah

as he has been every year for Chanukah since 1997.

This book is the result of his fascination with this

important chapter in American history the First Jews

ever to arrive in North America and his goal

their story be far more widely known.

This classic office tower 11 Broadway opened in 1896 defines

Bowling Green in its own way with its majestic presence. Much

history has taken place on this site long before beginning

with the earliest settlers who arrived. This is where

"Finding The Light" was written.

CLOSING WORDS

SO WHAT ABOUT THE FUTURE ??

As I complete this manuscript in June 2021, here in New York State the pandemic has been officially declared over. With all the suffering and death Covid-19 was responsible and continues to be around the world my personal experience has been nuanced. I suffered a somewhat severe bout of Covid-19 back in April 2020 but at the same time I have experienced a particularly productive creative period since recovering from Covid-19 up until the present. I have completed and published two books I had wanted to do. This will be my third this year. I hope to publish a fourth by December. Each to no surprise I consider important and useful each in a very different way.

As for the larger issues of Bowling Green its past, present and future, its most impressive history and very notably the arrival of the First Jews in North America right here and the celebration of the very first Chanukah in America at Bowling Green as I portray my story "Finding The Light" the focal point and basis for my writing this book, I hope the future of Chanukah here, and more generally of Lower Manhattan, New York City and the United States is far brighter than it has ever been ever before if we will all make it so.

A potentially all important basis and goal for doing so within sight but far enough in the future 5 years from now to do so is the 250th anniversary of American Independence in 2026 and this time far more inclusive than ever.

ABOUT THE AUTHOR

Arthur Piccolo first arrived at Bowling Green when he worked at One White-hall Street in the early 1980s. As so many others did in the warm months he came to enjoy Bowling Green Park at lunchtime. Unlike many others he learned the unique and long history of Bowling Green and as a result his serious interest in it and the surrounding Lower Manhattan.

This led to the first Christmas Tree ever at Bowling Green in December 1986, followed by the creation of the Bowling Green Association in 1988, and his ever deeper involvement in the area and a year round annual series of events every year since as well as the improvement of the area including installation of the first permanent lighting in Bowling Green Park.

A major development took place in December 1989 when the author convinced the late Italian American sculptor Arturo DiModica to bring his larger than life 3 ½ ton bronze "Charging Bull" to Bowling Green then make this world famous work a permanent gift to always remain at and be publicly displayed at the northern tip of Bowling Green for the enjoyment of millions.

Another significant enhancement took place in March 1996 when the Greek American community at the author's urging agreed to donate a second tower-ing 55 ft. flagpole to Bowling Green and as a result these last 25 years the flags of many nations have flown here beside the 13 star original American flag. The following year 1997 witnessed the first Menorah ever erected at Bowling Green an impressive sculpture by Arturo DiModica.

Bowling Green where New York City was founded as New Amsterdam remains the heart and soul of New York City at the center of the city's most impressive plaza, and the work of the Bowling Green Association continues under the leadership of Arthur Piccolo and this book being one new result.